# LOST IN THE OCEAN OF AGILITY

## by René Schröder

## About the author

René Schröder is at the forefront of the agile revolution, a master of change with a remarkable ability to weave agility into the backbone of organisations. With over two decades of experience, he pulls customised strategies for various industries out of his sleeve and transforms challenges into success stories. His approach is pragmatic, always focussing on the uniqueness of each company.

As the author of "The Panda Story" trilogy and an experienced conference speaker, René Schröder offers a mixture of wisdom and motivational rhetoric. His presence on stage awakens aspirations, his publications are signposts through the thicket of corporate complexity.

In agile consulting, René Schröder is an architect of customised solutions that shape and adapt teams and structures to meet the ever-changing demands of the business world. Clear vision, pragmatic implementation and measurable success characterise his partnership with companies embarking on the journey to agile excellence.

| | |
|---|---|
| Twitter | |
| Instagram | |
| Youtube | |
| LinkedIn | |
| Blog | |

# LOST IN THE OCEAN OF AGILITY

Sailing against the current
How to break through the fog of agility
and stay on course

René Schröder

1st edition, 50.2023
© 2023 Author: René Schröder
Illustrations: René Schröder
Translation: Julia Schröder
Proofreading: Gasha
Bookcover: Valentina P.
- All rights reserved.

RegSus Consulting GmbH, Munich
r.schroeder@regsus.de

# Contents

# CONTENTS

# Dedication

To my beloved wife Julia,

Your unceasing support, your wisdom and your unconditional love are the compass that guides me through the stormiest of waters. In the countless hours I have spent immersing myself in the depths of agility, you have been my anchor, keeping me firmly grounded in reality while filling my sails with inspiration and courage. Without your strength and understanding, this journey into the unknown would not have been possible. You are more than my life partner; you are the silent force behind every word I write.

To my children, Jason and Jasmin,

You are the stars in my darkest night, always reminding me why I embarked on this journey in the first place. Your childlike curiosity and unbridled optimism have always reminded me that the greatest adventure is not in discovering new worlds, but in seeing the world through your eyes. Your laughter and joy are my daily reminder that the true treasure of life is hidden in the little moments we spend together.

With love and gratitude

# Foreword by Javier Rodriguez Gonzalez

As a leader of a global advisory business, I have had the privilege of working with a wide variety of clients across a multitude of industries in different regions of the world. Having myself experienced different cultures in several countries, and having undergo several downs and highs of the global capital market have all provided me with a broad and deep understanding of today's businesses challenges, opportunities and common traps.

Throughout my career I have been dedicated to the pursuit of knowledge, understanding different perspectives and complementing my own views with those of experts in other disciplines and other ways of solving problems. In that context, I met René Schröder few years ago. I proudly consider him today a dear friend and an outstanding professional, therefore I am particularly excited to write the foreword of his latest book "Lost in the Ocean of Agility".

In my current role, I support numerous international corporations and private capital firms in navigating the stormy seas of continuously changing markets, shifting technologies and increasingly complex human organizations. The principles and insights described in this book reflect the real-life situations that current businesses face, abandoning purely theoretical frameworks and focusing on implementing agility as a way to transform the way you look at the market, your product and your people. The metaphor of the "3 paths to happiness" encompasses behaviors that I have too often seen in the market, those of companies holding to outdated solution maps, trying to piece together a ship starting from the disparate pieces they have at hand,

and sailing into the night with no clear direction or destination.

"Lost in the Ocean of Agility" not only provides a throughout analysis of the pitfalls in which organizations walk when undergoing their journey to agility, but rather provides practical strategies and implementable solutions that I would consider essential to achieve real lasting change and tangible results. The ability to "dance in the storm", as René puts it, is an art difficult to master that is usually characteristic of great leaders that achieve success over and over again, abandoning the excruciating governance controls of today´s organizations and cultivating instead a culture of adaptability, resilience and continuous learning. For as the market becomes more convoluted, complex and fast-changing, the solution can certainly not be to implement tighter and more prescriptive frameworks, but instead to adapt faster and less traumatically to new circumstances. Smile in the storm, for your skills is that of rough waters and agile ships.

I have experienced myself how implementing the ideas described in this book has helped organizations not only to survive, but most importantly to thrive in the age of change, by embracing the natural unpredictability of the market and by using it in their own advantage. "Lost in the Ocean of Agility" is therefore more than a business read, it is an essential guide for anyone wanting to grow in today's volatile business world, not by operating tighter than others but by becoming better at developing the right product, at the right time for the right customer.

I do heartfeltly recommend this book to all leaders and organizations embarking in the, sometimes scary and always well-worthy, journey of agile transformation. May you use the insights and strategies described in this book useful in charting your own course , and may you navigate the waves of change leading you to your desired destination.

I leave you with one of my favorite quotes when starting a transformation journey, one that usually sets the leadership team in the right direction: "The secret of change is to focus all your energy not on fighting the old, but on building the new", Socrates.

Hope you enjoy the read as much as I did, and thanks to my dear friend René for letting me write these words, you are and you will always be a beacon of agility shinning in a world of immutability, and an extraordinary person to be around.

**Best regards**
*Javier Rodriguez*
*Global Head of Value Creation, KPMG*
*International*

## FOREWORD BY JAVIER RODRIGUEZ GONZALEZ

# Introduction

Welcome aboard the "Agility", the ship that will guide us through the stormy waters of modern business life. I am René Schröder, your captain on this voyage, and I invite you to set sail with me on a voyage of discovery that will change the way you think, work and lead forever.

You, the brave navigators of the business world, the executives, project managers and teams who are not satisfied with the status quo, are in the right place. You are the innovators and pioneers who are ready to unfold the old maps and explore new horizons. They know that true agility is more than just a buzzword - it's a way of life, an art to be mastered.

In my book "Lost in the Ocean of Agility", I take you on a journey through the three paths of agility. We will leave behind the precise maps that promise an illusion of control; we will overcome the composite ship, the Wolpertinger, built out of despair and false assumptions; and we will expose the secret expedition that is driven more by hope than clarity.

Prepare to dive into the depths of agile philosophy, where you will learn that the real treasure is not the achievement of a fixed goal, but the journey itself. It is a journey full of lessons that will teach you to dance with the waves instead of fighting them.

This book is more than a collection of pages; it is a compass for those who are ready to weigh anchor and set course for a world where agility is the rudder that steers us through the stormy seas of change. Are you ready to sail with me into this exciting future? Then come on board and let's set sail together.

**Kind regards**
*René Schröder*

# Structure of the book

In "Lost in the Ocean of Agility", I take you on a journey that is structured to help you understand not only the theory behind agility, but also how to put it into practice. The book is divided into four main parts that guide you through the different aspects of agile transformation.

### Part I: The three paths to (in)agility

Here we explore the metaphorical paths that organisations often take when embarking on the journey of agility. We will analyse the pros and cons of each path and understand why some strategies lead astray while others lead to real progress.

### Part II: The maritime odyssey of precise maps

In this section, we'll dive deep into the first path - the quest for perfection through detailed planning. I'll show you why an excess of control can be just as dangerous as none at all and how to find a balance between preparation and flexibility.

## Part III: The Wolpertinger - A ship of myths

The second path leads us to a ship built from the best parts of other ships - or at least that's what they say. We will explore the pitfalls of solutions that are too unique to be true and how to develop a strategy that really fits your organisation.

## Part IV: The secret expedition - Navigating in the dark

The third path is the most mysterious. Here we look at organisations that set off into agility without a clear direction or understanding of the destination. I will show strategies on how to lead from this darkness into the light and create an environment where everyone in the team knows how and why decisions are made.

### Closing: Dancing up a storm

At the end of the book, we summarise the findings and look at the art of "dancing in the storm" - how to live and breathe agility. I will present concrete steps and methods that will help you not only to implement agility, but to make it an integral part of your corporate culture.

# The 3 paths to happiness?

In the endless seas of the market, where storms appear unexpectedly and success is as fleeting as a sun-drenched morning, companies have realised that they need to set their sails differently. The old methods, once as reliable as beacons on familiar shores, are no longer enough to navigate the rough waters of customer demands and competition.

**The first path** - a journey with maps on which every wind and every current is plotted, an odyssey so precisely orchestrated that nothing is left to chance. It is the illusion of control, the promise of safety, that if only every wave, every gust of wind is predictable, the ship will inevitably reach its harbour of destination. But the sea is capricious, and no plan, however detailed, can foresee the imponderables of every moment on the open water.

**The second path** is a ship, assembled like a Wolpertinger, a mythical creature of seafaring, born out of desperation and the false assumption that only a unique piece can weather the storms. Disparate parts from other ships, with no understanding of how they strengthen the whole, are joined together. It is a path that promises to be unique, to offer a solution, built on the idea that only that which is special and customised can be successful. Yet without a true understanding of the craft that is shipbuilding, it is nothing more than a floating nightmare, ready to break apart at the first wave.

And then there is **the third path** - a secret expedition, a crew left in the dark while their commanders mumble parts of the first and second path as if they were prayers to the gods of the sea. They sail, but blindly, unaware that the ship they are on has no true direction, no map worth following, only whispers and orders, held in the silence that inspires more fear than trust.

Why do these paths lead to disaster? Because they do not understand or honour the unpredictability of the human spirit, the chaos of creativity and innovation, the wild, untameable nature of the market itself. They try to chart stars that are constantly moving, to tame a sea that refuses to be tamed.

The true journey - the successful voyage - lies in understanding that the sea, as unpredictable as it is, must be experienced as it comes. You have to learn to dance in the storm instead of trying to avoid it, be willing to change your rudder based on what the waves tell you, not what the charts dictate.

It means seeing the crew as more than mere recipients of orders, allowing them to be part of the ship itself, putting their hands and hearts into the construction and navigation. It means seeing the journey as an experience, an adventure - uncertain, yes, but full of possibilities.

The sea of entrepreneurship cannot be controlled, but it can be experienced, in all its raw beauty and unpredictable tides. It is the brave, those who learn to sail with the unknown, who not only survive but truly live, leaving their stories in the stars that light up the night sky for those who have yet to sail.

## The first path - The maritime odyssey of precise maps

Imagine a proud ship setting sail in the early hours of the morning, when the first rays of sunlight colour the haze of the horizon golden. This is no ordinary ship, but the flagship of a proud trading empire preparing to discover a new world. ReG Inc. sees itself in this magnificent ship, ready to plunge into the uncharted waters of transformation.

But before this journey begins, every mile of the ocean is meticulously surveyed in the company's cartography chambers. Every gust of wind is predicted, every wave is known, and every storm is marked on the charts, which are so detailed that they even document the song of the mermaids in the depths. These nautical charts are not just a plan - they are a promise, a guarantee that nothing will be left to chance. The leaders, the cartographers, have counted every grain of sand on the seabed and are convinced that their precise calculations and predictions will guide them safely through the stormiest waters.

The ship casts off and the entire board is on deck, eyes firmly fixed on the clearly defined horizon. The crew, the employees, stand at attention and ready, because they trust in the wisdom of their admirals and the precision of their charts. They believe that every storm, every headwind will only be a minor inconvenience on an otherwise flawlessly planned voyage.

But the sea, just like the market, is a living beast. It ripples and rages with unforeseen ferocity, and soon the proud ship is shaken by turbulence that was not on the charts. Storms are brewing, not where they were expected, but where the cartographers had clearly drawn the skies. Unknown currents, metaphorical for unexpected market changes, tear at the keel, and the beautiful lines of the nautical charts begin to fade, soaked by the splashing salt water of reality.

The crew begins to get nervous, looking questioningly at their leaders, who stoically try to hide their uncertainty as they redraw their maps in the midst of chaos they had not foreseen. In their arrogance, they had believed that nature, like the market, follows a linear logic, a predictable formula that they only had to decipher in order to reach their destination safely.

In this maelstrom of events, a few brave souls on board realise that no map, no matter how accurate, could ever capture the living, breathing volatility of the ocean. They begin to take the helm by listening to their instincts, their experience and their understanding of the sea they have travelled through.

ReG Inc's journey, this path of fully planned transformation, is no longer a journey but a battle - a battle, not against the sea, but against the illusion of predictability and control. As they grapple with the unpredictable nature of the market, they learn that no journey, especially one of transformation, is a straight line route from point A to point B. It is an odyssey that requires adaptability, courage and a willingness to crumple up the maps and be led by the winds of change.

## The second path - The Wolpertinger ship

The second path that ReG Inc. could take resembles a jumbled ship reminiscent of the legendary Wolpertinger - a hybrid of various creatures that takes on bizarre and unexpected forms in folklore. In this scenario, the company has put together pieces of various agile frameworks, a bit of Scrum here, a bit of Kanban there, some principles of Lean and perhaps even elements of Extreme Programming. Each piece has been selected in the hope of inheriting the agility, efficiency or some other attractive feature promised by the respective framework.

But like a Wolpertinger at sea, this ship is not made from a single mould. It was born out of desperation and the deluded belief that a purely unique, customised vehicle - free from the 'constraints' of traditional, tried and tested designs - would be better equipped to navigate the stormy seas of the market. Management mistakenly believes that this Frankensteinian creation of agile methodologies would provide a stronger, more resilient structure as it combines "the best of all worlds".

However, this approach lacks a fundamental understanding of how these different methods and principles should work together synergistically. There is a lack of realisation that each agile framework - like each part of the ship - was developed within a specific context, with specific requirements that it fulfils and specific problems that it addresses. By randomly assembling pieces without guidance or strategy, management risks not only the integrity of their "ship", but also the direction and progress of their journey.

This composite "ship" may impress at first glance with its unconventional design and apparent uniqueness. It promises a customised solution, an answer to all the challenges the company faces. But without a true understanding of naval architecture, that is, without a deep, nuanced understanding of how agile principles can be successfully integrated and applied, this ship is not seaworthy. It is a floating nightmare that, instead of cutting through the waves, threatens to break up at the first encounter with difficulty.

This approach, which focuses on uniqueness and customisation without taking into account the need for understanding and coherence, can lead the company into dangerous waters. It runs the risk of wasting resources, demoralising the team and ultimately preventing the company from achieving its true goals. The lesson here is clear: true seaworthiness - and true business success - does not come from a "random" set of concepts, but rather comes from continuously generating experience within the organisation and following the Shu-Ha-Ri principle.

## The third path - The secret expedition

The third path, an odyssey that is more like a nightmarish riddle than a journey, draws its travellers into a maelstrom of secrets and uncertainties. It is as if a courageous crew boards a ship that is steered not by an experienced captain, but by shadows and echoes. This expedition, shrouded in darkness, hides its true destination from those brave enough to set sail, trapping their hearts in a web of whispers and hidden agendas.

From the outset, this ship - this fragile ark in the infinite sea of the corporate world - is a conglomeration of parts of the first and second path. It is as if the architects have taken a little bit of everything, but without the glue of understanding that could hold these disparate elements together. The leaders, the commanders of this daring endeavour, mumble fragments of strategies they barely understand, as if they were sacred incantations meant to appease the raging sea gods. But these unclear messages serve more to fan the flames of uncertainty burning in the hearts of their crew.

The crew members, the brave souls on this enigmatic ship, are sailing on a sea without a horizon. They feel the deck sway beneath their feet with every decision made more out of fear than trust. The silence in which they are held is oppressive - a world in which even the creaking of the ship sounds like a sigh of resignation. Their gazes often meet in the blackness of the night, their eyes full of questions to which no one seems to have an answer.

In this atmosphere of half-truths and assumptions, the course they are following is nothing more than an illusion. The maps they have are blank sheets of paper, lines and paths drawn by an invisible hand and just as quickly wiped away again. There is no lighthouse in the distance, no promise of a safe harbour - just the endless wavering and the occasional, fright-filled flicker of hope that is quickly smothered by the next wave of confusion.

In this world of half-shadows and unspoken mistrust, the journey itself becomes a metaphor for the loss and silent despair that everyone carries in their hearts. It is a journey without a destination, a quest without a promise, a siren song that inexorably pulls the ship and its crew into the depths of the unknown and unexplored ocean.

## The odyssey of transformation in three acts

In the unfathomable depths of the entrepreneurial ocean, we have seen three ships, each on a course to destruction, marked by the trials and tribulations of poorly navigated strategies. The first path, a mighty ship that met its demise through hubris and lack of reflection, reflected the danger of relying solely on theoretical knowledge without supplementing it with practical application. The second path, a bizarre patchwork of methods pulled from various corners and ends without understanding or context, showed us that without a solid foundation and respect for the stages of learning - Shu Ha Ri - no sustainable progress is possible. The third path, a journey led through the darkness of not knowing and uncertainty, painfully reminded us how a lack of clear goals and decentralised decision making can lead an organisation astray.

But from the wreckage of these failed expeditions, a map for success is emerging. For those who have chosen the first path, salvation lies in merging thought and action. It is time to bridge the gap between theory and practice to develop an understanding that is grounded in the real world of business. Leaders need to come on deck, feel the wind in their sails and work alongside their crew to truly understand the nuances of their ship.

Those who are lost on the second, chaotic path must embrace the philosophy of Shu Ha Ri to achieve true mastery. They must realise that true expertise requires more than a smorgasbord of concepts; it requires a progressive journey from imitation to assimilation to innovation. Experience, they will learn, is not just a function of knowledge, but of lived, felt and experienced understanding.

For the unfortunate souls on the third path, the reversal of their course is required through the courage to make decentralised decisions, empowering the crew to take the helm. Shifting the focus from mere output to meaningful outcome will not only move the ship forward but also in the right direction.

The sea of business is full of uncertainties, but for those who are willing to learn from their mistakes and adapt to the tides, there is always hope on the horizon. A world awaits where businesses not only survive, but thrive; a future where teams work together not out of necessity, but out of a shared pursuit of excellence; and a destination where success is defined not by reaching the shore, but by the journey you take, the challenges you overcome and the discoveries you make along the way.

# A new horizon ~ The three paths out of the labyrinth of uniformity

In a world that is constantly changing, companies are faced with a labyrinth of uniformity in which old maps and compass needles can no longer point the way. However, there are paths that lead out of this labyrinth - three paths out that show the brave and wise a new direction.

## The first path out: The maritime odyssey of precise maps

Here the journey begins with the realisation that the old maps no longer reflect the truth of the sea. It is a journey that teaches us that true navigation requires a willingness to redraw the maps - not with ink, but with an understanding of the currents of the market and the winds of change.

## The second path out: Of wolpertingers and sea masters ~ The odyssey to agile mastery

This path leads us through the philosophy of Shu Ha Ri, where true mastery lies not in rigid imitation, but in fluid adaptation and ultimately in creative innovation. It is a path that shows us how to step out of the shadows of convention and into the light of realisation.

## The third path out: The secret expedition ~ From the shadow of the third path

The last resort leads us to the hidden expeditions that have freed themselves from the shackles of the so-called "third path". It is a path that teaches us that true change lies not in the numbers and data we measure, but in the stories and experiences we create.

These three paths out are more than just escape routes from stagnation; they are invitations to a journey that leads us not only to a new place, but to a new way of being. They challenge us not only to think differently, but to live differently - in a world that no longer revolves around the 'what', but around the 'why' and the 'how'.

Join us on this journey to the three paths out that will not only transform our companies, but also our souls.

## How the maritime odyssey of precise maps came to an end

A sailboat, embedded in the waters of unpredictability, discovers that the first road to disaster is often a map full of deceptions. It is the map of over-planning and over-cautious navigation, drawn with the inkwell of the illusion that every mile, every gust of wind, every change in current is predictable, controllable. Companies that hold this map believe that they can traverse the oceans of transformation with a precisely defined route, ignoring the capricious waves of change.

But the sea of change is a living, breathing entity, untamed and unpredictable. It dances to the beat of the tides, seduced by the whims of the moon, and any ship attempting to chart its paths finds itself entangled in a web of waves and currents that take no heed of human plans. The assumption that the transformation is a calm sea, ready to bend to the will of compass and sextant, is a dangerous marine illusion. In reality, it is a stormy ocean that hurls boats into uncharted waters where monsters wait and sirens sing.

In the 21st century, the world has thrown off the shackles of predictability and turned into a wild sea characterised by networks of dependencies and waves of technology. The winds of globalisation have created new currents that turn into turbulent interactions, while technological progress, like a lighthouse, illuminates the cliffs of possibility, often without showing the course to the safe shore. In this ocean, old methods of navigation are not only inadequate, but often dangerous.

The centralisation of decisions, a relic of old seafaring traditions, shows its cracks in the face of the raging sea. The assumption that a captain, locked in his cabin, away from the decks and the salty spray, can make the best decisions is as ramshackle as a shipwreck. The truth lives in every sailor, in the hand that holds the wheel, in the eyes that recognise the storm on the horizon. It is a truth that manifests itself in the fusion of thought and action, in the spontaneous adaptation to the rhythm of the waves.

Decentralised structures awaken this spirit by handing over the helm to those who feel the foam of the waves at their fingertips. They foster a crew that breathes in unison with the sea, that is able to set sail on the winds of change, that not only reacts to storms but anticipates them, feels them long before they darken the horizon.

The old maps that were once considered indispensable are now fading. The ink with which they were written has run in the face of complexity. It is time to turn the wheel, change course and set sail into the tides of uncertainty with the confidence that the crew, when free, can navigate the ship through any storm. This maritime odyssey is not the end, but a new beginning, an invitation to embrace the oceans of possibility without fear of the uncertainties they harbour.

The maritime odyssey is a dance with the unknown, a bold leap into the depths of change where the only thing certain is the movement itself. It is a journey that 21st century businesses should not fear but celebrate, for in these uncharted waters we find not only challenges but also the untamed possibilities of the future.

## Sailing against the storm: How decentralised decision-making ships are navigating the tides of transformation

Imagine a mighty sailing ship, the kingdom of an old and proud admiral who rules the sea. In traditional fashion, he directs from his captain's chair, high up on the top deck, seeing alone which way the wind is blowing and deciding which course to take. This ship represents centralised decision-making - one where every rope, every change of sail, every new course is ordered from this central, elevated position. It is a system of order, rank and unity, but also one that slowly follows the winds of change.

Now, in the dense fog of economic uncertainty and rapid change, this monolithic ship is faltering. The admiral's orders have to be laboriously relayed down through the ranks, from deck to deck, over loud megaphones and through a chain of messengers, until they finally reach the ears of the sailors hoisting the sails and operating the rudders. It is a slow dance, one that makes the ship sluggish and clumsy against the ever-changing winds of the sea.

Then there is the flotilla of agile, smaller ships that cruise the sea together. Each ship in this flotilla is a master of its own destiny, led by a captain who stands among the crew, feels the wind, tastes the salt and quickly changes course depending on how the wind blows and the current flows. These ships represent decentralised decision-making.

In this swarm of ships, in this agile flotilla, each ship is responsible for its own survival. They communicate quickly and efficiently with each other, warn each other of storms and divide the spoils among themselves. They are resilient, for while one ship may struggle, the rest remain strong and responsive, providing support and drawing lessons from the challenges of each.

In the world of transformation, it's like breaking up the proud hierarchy of the monolithic ship and transforming it into a fleet of agile, responsive vessels that traverse the sea with speed and determination. Where once the old admiral looked wearily down on his empire, there are now a multitude of captains making real-time decisions, adapting, collaborating and navigating the rough seas of market changes and customer needs.

This maritime revolution in decision-making is a crucial turning point in the seafaring history of the business world. It is a recognition that while the old, big ship may be majestic and imposing, it is the fast, manoeuvrable ships that are braving the storms, finding the treasures and sailing the future on the unpredictable waves of the market.

## Logbook entry

And so, our seafaring story ends, not with a calm breeze, but with a merry storm of laughter and realisation. As the old sea dogs would say: "A happy ship is a fast ship!" and in the world of business, this couldn't be truer.

In the rough seas of the corporate world, it is not the strongest or the biggest who survive, but the one who is prepared to turn the helm quickly, set sail in all directions and navigate the stormiest seas with a smile. It is the captains who laugh when the rain soaks them, who sing when the waves hit the deck and who dare to dance when the lightning lights up the night sky.

Centralisation? A stiff breeze that could tear the sail apart! Over-planning? A hidden reef waiting to destroy our proud ship of efficiency! No, in this odyssey of transformation, it is the dancing, laughing, improvising ships that reach the harbour, laden with the treasures of success and innovation.

So, proud leaders, throw away your cards, feel the wind in your hair and learn the joyful dance of agile navigation! Because at the end of the day, it's the joy that brings speed, the camaraderie that stabilises the rudder and the laughter that guides us through the darkest nights.

May our business flotilla continue to sail boldly where no monolith ship has ever succeeded. With a song in our hearts and a quick jig on our lips, we steer towards a future as vast and marvellous as the sea itself. Ahoy, captains of industry, and may your decisions be as swift and cheerful as the waves that herald our next great adventure!

# Of Wolpertingers and Sea Masters ~ The Odyssey to Agile Mastery

A ship shaped like a Wolpertinger, a chimera from the realm of fables, glides amidst the turbulent seas of the corporate world. It is cobbled together from fragments of various ships, a product of desperation and the deceptive conviction that only such a unique vessel could survive the raging storms. This ship symbolises companies that decide to forge their own methods because they believe that the tried and tested frameworks such as Scrum do not meet their unique challenges.

But ah, here lies a wild misunderstanding of agility, hidden deep in the planks of the Wolpertinger ship. Agility dances on the waves of experience and continuous improvement, it cannot be squeezed into a corset of rigid, home-made frameworks. Here, the living, breathing essence of experience is confused with the rigid skeleton of knowledge, resulting in a grotesque creature that is doomed to failure.

Knowledge, the golden fleece of scholars, inhabits the halls of our intellect, a collection of sparkling jewels - information, facts, concepts - acquired through study, observation or exchange. It is the land of theory, of strategies drawn on maps that have never felt the rough touch of the wind.

Experience, on the other hand, is like the old sea dog whose hands are marked by practice. It comes through action, through navigating the stormy seas, experiencing breezes and storms in equal measure. Experience is the touchstone of knowledge, the place where theories are tested for their suitability, where they can be broken, reforged and strengthened.

Here, between the cliffs of knowledge and the whirlpools of experience, we sail on the waves of Shu Ha Ri, a concept from the art of the samurai that shows the path from imitation to assimilation to innovation.

Shu: In the first phase, the "Shu" phase, we are faithful students of tradition. We follow established practices such as Scrum with respect and precision, learning the rules and sticking to them, just as the apprentice follows the movements of his master. This is where Scrum protects us from the storms of distraction and chaos by providing us with a safe harbour of structure.

Ha: As we move into the "Ha" phase, we begin to question and adopt the rules. Here, much like an adolescent sailor learning to stand on his own two feet, we begin to make our own decisions, still within the framework, but with greater understanding and adaptation to our unique journey. Scrum serves as our compass, pointing us in the right direction, but which we now interpret and adapt as we understand the winds and currents of our own organisational seas.

Ri: Finally, in the "Ri" phase, we become masters of our art. We break the rules, but with respect and understanding for their essence. Like experienced captains, we navigate our ship intuitively, no longer bound by textbooks, but free to change course as the current situation demands. Scrum is now a part of us, an inner compass, internalised and adapted to our needs.

The Wolpertinger ship, built without these principles, is doomed to fail. It is a floating nightmare, ready to break apart at the first wave. Companies must embark on the journey through Shu Ha Ri to become truly seaworthy. They must learn the craft from the bottom up, building their ships not out of misunderstanding and despair, but out of strength, understanding and adaptability. Only then can they successfully navigate the stormy seas of the business world and carry their valuable cargo safely across the raging waters of the market.

## A Scrum Wolpertinger

Shu Ha Ri, a philosophy that has its roots in traditional Japanese martial arts, can be metaphorically applied to the development of organisations and their approach to agile methods such as Scrum. It is a journey that takes the organisation from strict compliance to critical understanding to innovative self-reliance, much like a ship that is built and improved over time to meet the growing challenges of the open seas.

Shu (守: "preserve"): This initial phase is
comparable to building the hull of a ship, the
most fundamental part that keeps it afloat. In
this phase, companies strictly follow the
prescribed framework and methods as set out
in Scrum. They preserve tradition and best
practices to create a solid foundation. This is
not a time for a Wolpertinger ship; it is not a
time for wild experimentation with untested
parts or piecing together incongruent practices.
Just as a hull must be built to certain
specifications to be seaworthy, the approach to
agile methods at this stage must be precise
and unchanged to set the organisation on the
right course.

Ha (破: "to relieve"): When the ship - or in
this case the company - reaches the open sea
and encounters its first storms, the "Ha" phase
begins. This is when the deck, masts and sails
are established, but each element remains
adjustable. The companies have internalised

the rules and methods of Scrum and are now beginning to look at them critically. They understand not only how they do things, but also why. In this phase, parts of the "Wolpertinger ship" are allowed to emerge: innovative solutions and customisations that ride the waves of experience and understanding. However, these parts must be carefully selected and tested so as not to jeopardise the integrity of the ship. The company breaks away from rigid adherence to the rules and adapts its strategies to the unique challenges and conditions it encounters at sea.

Ri (離: "to separate"): Finally, when the ship has mastered the ocean and every part and seam has experienced storms and calm seas in equal measure, the "Ri" phase begins. The company has fully understood and integrated the agile methods; they have become part of its DNA. Now it is ready to "break away" from the rules and go its own way. The Wolpertinger ship is no longer a patchwork, but a customised masterpiece that builds on the previous phases. This is the time for creativity and innovation, the time to develop unique solutions that go beyond what existing frameworks prescribe. However, this freedom does not come from a lack of respect for tradition, but from a deep understanding and mastery of it.

The Wolpertinger ship that is born too early in the "Shu" phase is not seaworthy; it is a danger to itself. Only when the company goes through "Ha" and approaches the "Ri" phase is the Wolpertinger ship allowed to emerge in all its splendour and uniqueness, born of experience, understanding and a deep mastery of agile principles and practices. It then embodies not chaos, but harmonious innovation.

## Logbook entry

Ah, brave captains and skilful shipbuilders, let's put down the binoculars and take stock with a twinkle in our eyes. What a voyage it was, across the stormy seas of agility, full of mythical Wolpertinger ships that looked more like ships in bottles glued together in stormy seas.

We learned that assembling a ship from the most colourful and seemingly exotic parts - as tempting as it may seem - does not necessarily make us the proud owners of a seaworthy galleon. No, it only led us to a patchwork on the waves, ready to break apart at the first gust.

But then came Shu Ha Ri, shining like the North Star in the night sky, to show us the way. From the first phase, where we learnt the basics of shipbuilding (Shu), to experimenting with new materials and techniques (Ha), to mastering our craft, where we learnt to build our own unique ship (Ri) that would not only weather the storms, but dance elegantly through them.

So, what do we, captains of industry and masters of shipbuilding, take away from this journey? That the true path to mastery is through understanding, adapting and ultimately mastering the art of shipbuilding. A Wolpertinger may be a curiosity, but without a solid foundation and understanding of its design, it will never be more than a sculpture in the harbour.

The journey to agile mastery, gentlemen and ladies, is like discovering new continents: it is neither short nor easy, and certainly not without a leak or two in the hull. But with Shu Ha Ri as our compass and a smile in our hearts, we will not only learn to survive the storms, but to dance with them.

So may your Wolpertinger ships be transformed, from fragile curiosities to proud flagships of innovation. Set sail for new horizons, captains, and may the wind of agility always blow in your sails!

## The secret expedition ~ From the shadow of the third path

As if emerging from the mists of despair, there is a hidden expedition that has freed itself from the shackles of the so-called "third path". This path to disaster, characterised by a shadowy team posing as the guardians of change, had entrenched itself in the dark chambers of isolation. With plans as fragile as cobwebs, they attempted to capture the living essence of transformation, not realising that true change flows as freely as the wind itself.

But in this hidden expedition, far from the fatal halls of rigid thought and action, a new melody began to play. It was a symphony that echoed in the heart of each individual, a gentle awakening that consumed the shadows of the third path. This courageous collective, armed with the understanding that true transformation is born in the hallways of dialogue and unity, created a bridge across the divide that separated the architects of change from those who would carry their plans.

Moving away from the deceptive spotlight of outputs, which is only the illusion of progress, they turned to the soft glow of outcomes. This light, born of the deep desires and hopes of those they sought to serve, painted a picture not only of the work they did, but of the souls they touched, the lives they changed. It was not the number of steps they counted, but the footprints they left in the sands of time.

In this secret expedition, change was not seen as a declaration of war where strategies were wielded like swords. Instead, it was a dance, an invitation for everyone to hold hands and sway together to the rhythm of renewal. It was a process that was not amplified by the echoes of isolation, but by the harmony of hearts beating as one.

The cards they now had in front of them were no longer blank sheets of paper, drawn and erased by invisible hands. They were living works of art, changing with every breath, with lines drawn by the ink of experience, empathy and genuine encounter. Each path on this map had the potential to ignite a lighthouse in the distance, a promise of a harbour hidden in the collective soul of each individual.

So, this secret expedition sailed, no longer driven by the stormy winds of mistrust, but by the gentle breeze of hope. They understood that it was not the land they had to conquer, but the hearts of those who sailed with them. In this world of connected souls and shared dreams, their journey became not one of loss and silent despair, but a vibrant odyssey of change, love and infinite potential.

## In harmony with the horizon: the symphony of collective discovery

On the infinite sea of change, far removed from the old world of rigid output, a ship glides gently over the waves of change. It is no ordinary ship, but a community of explorers whose eyes are firmly fixed on the horizon - on the discovery of a new continent, the Outcome.

On board this ship there is no autocrat, no single captain who hurls down orders like lightning bolts from a hidden cloud. Here, under the vast skies of possibility, every sailor, every navigator, every man and woman is part of a fluid hierarchy based on the expertise and insight that each moment demands.

Collaboration begins with the shared knowledge of the goal - the green shores of the new continent. This goal, as clear as the midday sun above the mast, illuminates every task, every contribution. Everyone knows why they set the sails, why they tighten the lines, why they watch through the darkness at night. It is not the frequency of the rowing strokes that counts, but the shared understanding that every stroke brings them closer to the coast, that every gentle glide over a wave means a gentle approach to the goal.

Instead of working to the beat of a prescribed order, the rowing crew feel the speed of the sea and intuitively adjust their strokes. They know that it is not the speed with which they row, but the interplay of their forces and their understanding of the currents that will propel them forward effectively. Their coordination is a dance on the water, a ballet in which every rowing stroke is an expression of collective endeavour.

The navigators, freed from the confines of command and control, share their wisdom with the crew. They not only plot courses on maps, but also inspire with tales of what lies beyond the horizon. They keep an eye out for signs of the weather, for the stars in the night sky, and pass on their findings so that everyone knows and understands the direction.

Communication is the water that feeds the ship's lifelines. It flows openly and freely, nourishing every decision and every exchange of ideas. Instead of orders, there are dialogues; instead of rules, there are agreements. The ship is not steered by the authority of one individual, but by the collective intelligence of all the souls on board.

And so, in the vast ocean of transition, this ship sails ahead, carried by the winds of shared vision. Each member of the crew contributes equally to the destination, bringing individual strengths while honouring the shared journey. The destination, the new continent, is not just a physical place they hope to reach, but a symbol of their shared values and hopes, of a future they want to shape together.

When the ship finally crosses the silver line of the new continent, it is not the arrival of an individual who sets foot there, but the awakening of an entire community that is entering a new world together.

## Logbook entry

And there we have it, dear viewers, the dramatic climax of our little nautical story. At the end of the day, when the last ray of sunlight disappears behind the horizon and the sea spray mixes with the starlight, we see clearly: the game of output versus outcome is like trying to measure the sea with a fishing net - you catch a few fish, but the sea remains unfathomable.

We learnt that breaking the old chains of separation between thought and action was not a quiet endeavour - oh no! It was like throwing a message in a bottle into an orchestra pit and waiting for the symphony to begin. A symphony in which every musician not only knows their notes, but also understands how their melody contributes to the greater whole.

The captain, who used to be a tyrannical timekeeper who dictated every stroke of the oars, is now more of a leading conductor in an orchestra where everyone knows their own notes. The crew, once mere pieces on the chessboard of the sea, are now bold explorers who understand that the rhythm of their oar strokes is more than just movement - it is poetry in action.

And so, with a wink and a smile, our heroes sail towards the new continent, no longer as prisoners of a secret expedition, but as part of a community that knows that the real treasure lies not in the number of kilometres rowed, but in the interwoven stories of every soul on board.

The ship may have left the harbour with a plan, but it will return with a legend. A legend that tells how the interplay of hand and spirit, of output and outcome, of a ship and its crew, has sailed the infinite sea of possibilities. Not as slaves to a stubbornly fixed course, but as friends sailing together against the wind in search of a goal that is greater than the sum of all maps, compass directions and star constellations - the goal of a shared future.

So, let's weigh anchor and set sail, because in this world of infinite possibilities, the journey itself is the greatest treasure, and the laughter we share along the way is the echo of our success. Cheers, to the journey!

# Last logbook entry ~ Conclusion of the journey: The synthesis of the Three paths

Today marks the end of our epic journey through the stormy waters of transformation and change. We have travelled the Three Paths of Knowledge and explored the Three paths Out that have led us out of the labyrinth of sameness. Here is a summary of our discoveries:

## The three paths to happiness

The maritime odyssey of precise maps taught us that true navigation requires a willingness to redraw the maps again and again, based on the ever-changing realities of the market.

The Wolpertinger ship took us through the philosophy of Shu Ha Ri, where we learnt that mastery lies in adaptation and innovation, not in rigid imitation.

The secret expedition revealed that true change is not in the numbers we measure, but in the stories we tell and the experiences we enable.

## The three paths out of the labyrinth of uniformity

The maritime odyssey of precise charts showed us that over-planning and over-control can lead us astray. We have to learn to sail in harmony with the unpredictable.

Of Wolpertingers and Sea Masters - Understanding Shu Ha Ri Better encouraged us to go beyond the mere application of methods to a deeper, intuitive connection with our practices.

From the Shadow of the Third path taught us that the true value of our work lies not in quantifiable outputs, but in the outcomes that enrich the lives of the people we work for.

As we have explored these paths and ways out, we have learnt that our journey never really ends. Each horizon leads to a new one, and with each sunrise we set sail again, enriched by the knowledge and experiences of the previous day.

We have learnt that transformation is a journey that leads both inwards and outwards. It is a dance between what we know and what we are yet to discover. It is an ongoing conversation between who we were yesterday and who we will be tomorrow.

With these realisations, we close this logbook, ready for the adventures that lie

ahead and grateful for the wisdom we have
gathered along the way.

# More expeditions to follow
# The journey continues with the 3R

Having travelled the three paths of knowledge and explored the three pas out of the labyrinth of uniformity, we are now at the beginning of a new chapter in thour journey. The next stage leads us to the 3Rs - the right product, at the right time, right for the customer. This outlook is intended to prepare us for the challenges and opportunities that lie ahead.

## The right product

Our journey has taught us that it is not enough to create products that merely exist. We need to develop products that resonate, that respond to the deepest needs and desires of our customers. The 3R method challenges us not only to build what we can, but to create what is needed - products that not only work, but inspire.

## At the right time

Timing is everything. Like the tides of the sea and the phases of the moon, we must learn to sense the rhythm of the market and adjust our sails accordingly. The right time for a product means capturing the moment when demand and readiness intersect. It is about feeling the pulse of the times and acting in perfect time.

## Right with the customer

The last R wisdom teaches us that our journey does not end when the product leaves the harbour walls. It continues until it is safely in the hands of those for whom it is intended. Getting it right with the customer means that our products not only arrive, but that they are also accepted, appreciated and used. It's about creating a connection that goes beyond the transactional and creates real value.

The 3Rs are the natural next step on our journey. They build on the insights of the Three Ways and Paths and lead us to a place where our products not only exist, but live - in the hands and hearts of our customers. With the 3Rs as our compass, we are setting our sails for a future where success is measured not just by sales figures, but by genuine customer satisfaction and lasting impact.

Let us explore this new horizon together, with the lessons we have learnt and the wisdom we are yet to gain. Onwards to the 3Rs - onwards to a future that we shape together.

**With anticipation of what is to come,**
*René Schröder*

## Previous expeditions

 "Follow ... the path of Ray, Howard, and Britta" - A compass through the world of agile transformation.

Set sail for an adventure of a special kind with René Schröder's book "Follow ... the path of Ray, Howard, and Britta". In this captivating work, you become part of a crew that embarks on a journey through the choppy waters of agile transformation. With each page, a story unfolds that conveys not only the principles of Scrum and agility, but also the human challenges and triumphs that come with real change.

The journey begins with the refinement of user stories, navigates through the depths of retrospectives and DoR, and steers through the challenges of sprint lengths and goals. Like an experienced helmsman who knows the winds of the market, Schröder guides you through the complex scenarios that can arise in the agile world - from the threat of escalation to the triumph of a successful click dummy.

Each episode is a chapter in itself, enriching the agile clinic with practical tips and reflections. You'll witness how Ray, Howard and Britta wrestle with the approach to an important trade show, how communication and collaboration tip the scales for success, and how the role of the product owner becomes crucial when it comes to setting sail in the right direction.

This book is more than a collection of stories. It is a navigation tool that shows you how to successfully shape your agile journey by asking the right questions and making the right decisions. It is a reflection of the reality of many organisations that have embarked on the agile journey, learning to deal with uncertainty and learning from mistakes.

If you're ready to weigh anchor and dive into the world of agility, then "Follow ... the path of Ray, Howard, and Britta" is your perfect companion. It is a book that not only informs, but also inspires and invites you to become part of the crew that steers the course to success together.

## A call to crew ~ Let your voice set sail on Amazon

Sailors and explorers of agility,

After navigating the turbulent waters of "Lost in the Ocean of Agility", you are now at the helm of a ship full of knowledge and insights. It's time to share your experiences and shine a light for other sailors on their journey to agile mastery. Your review on Amazon is like a lighthouse in the night - guiding and inspiring others who are venturing into similar waters.

Why your navigation stars (reviews) are
important

- **Compass for future explorers:** your
  thoughts illuminate the path for others
  who want to embark on their own
  agile journey.

- **Course correction for our next
  expedition:** Your insights are
  valuable to refine the maps and make
  future editions even more navigable.

- **Community of discovery:** Share
  your discoveries and become part of a
  crew of like-minded people committed
  to agility and transformation.

How to set your rating sails on Amazon

1. **Drop anchor on Amazon:** Head to your browser or the Amazon app.
2. **On course for the book:** Search for "Lost in the ocean of agility" and open the book page.
3. **Find the port of reviews:** Scroll down to the "Customer Reviews" section.
4. **Set the stars in the sky:** choose between 1 (hardly any wind) and 5 (full sail) stars for your review.
5. **Tell your story:** Click on "Write a review". Describe your journey with the book - what lit your way, what storms could have been avoided?
6. **Your message in a bottle:** Check your review and then send it on its way.

Thank you for being part of this great expedition. Your words are like the wind in our sails - pushing us and other brave souls forward as we venture into the unknown sea of agility.

**With adventurous greetings**

*René Schröder*